DRUMMING UP AN APPETITE

WITH

VINNIE PAUL

COOKING HOSTILE WITH THE PANTERA/DAMAGEPLAN/HELLYEAH LEGEND

WRITTEN BY
VINNIE PAUL

PUBLISHER	Sridhar Reddy
CHIEF EXECUTIVE OFFICER	Kevin Meek
PRESIDENT	Josh Bernstein
EDITOR IN CHIEF	Rantz A. Hoseley
V.P., OPERATIONS	Thomas Dreux
V.P., BUSINESS DEVELOPMENT	Anthony Lauletta
EDITOR	Jasminne Saravia
MARKETING MANAGER	Geri Imbriani
ART DIRECTOR	Rob Schwager
CUSTOMER SERVICE DIRECTOR	Gabriel Rosés
MARKETING DESIGNER	Darren Vogt
MANAGEMENT	Kimberly Zide Davis for Mike Davis Productions, Inc.

DRUMMING UP AN APPETITE

WITH

VINNIE PAUL

COOKING HOSTILE WITH THE PANTERA/DAMAGEPLAN/HELLYEAH LEGEND

COVER ART
ERIK RODRIGUEZ

PHOTOGRAPHY
JUSTIN BORUCKI

FOOD STYLING
DANIELLE HORNER

DESIGN
MICHAEL WILSON + JOSH BERNSTEIN

FOREWORD
CARROT TOP

AFTERWORD
BRIAN JONES

ILLUSTRATIONS
DANNY HELLMAN + STEVE CHANKS

EDITOR
JOSH BERNSTEIN

CONTENTS

CHAPTER 3:

DIETARY KEY

Contains Gluten

Vegetarian

Some diners may find this recipe SPICY!!!

Contains Dairy

ONE OF THE PERKS OF BEING IN THE ENTERTAINMENT BUSINESS

IS GETTING TO MEET OTHER ENTERTAINERS. I'VE BEEN LUCKY TO MEET ALL SORTS OF ROCK STARS, MOVIE STARS, TV STARS, PRO ATHLETES, COMEDIANS, MAGICIANS, AND MORE. MOST OF THEM ARE JUST AS HAPPY TO MEET ME AS I AM THEM. SOMETIMES, YOU BECOME FRIENDLIER WITH THEM WITH SOME BECOMING GENUINE FRIENDS. THEN THERE ARE THE FEW SPECIAL ONES THAT BECOME MORE LIKE FAMILY. THIS IS ABOUT ONE OF THEM.

I first met Vinnie Paul when he came to the show years ago, maybe 2006. My crew and I ha great time with him and his crew backstage. He seemed to genuinely like the show. As th years progressed, he came to the show more and more, always laughing like it was the firs time. He loved talking about the small changes or minor tweaks to some of the classic joke as well as new ones. Yeah, he was a legit rock star, but, he genuinely loved coming to th show. Over the years, he came to 350+ shows.

He wound up buying a house here in Las Vegas, close by the strip. It was a perfect house for him. He loved "The Casa". He started having people over all the time and would have a great spread. But, there was nothing like the spreads he'd go all out for on Sundays. That was Sunday Funday! Didn't matter what time of year, when he was in Vegas, it was ON! He would go all out for it. No matter how late Saturday night was, he was up early on Sundays shopping for the party. Those were some of the best days. There was almost anything you could imagine on the buffet. He would make steaks, chicken, hot dogs, burgers, chili, corn, potatoes, veggies, meatballs, poppers, and much more. When it was holiday season, the house would be decorated and the food would be holiday themed as well. During foot-ball season, it wasn't uncommon for him to prep food for his beloved Dallas Cowboys, but he'd make stuff from the other team as well. What I didn't know at the time was that almost everything he made was from his recipes. He loved having everyone over for a party, and you never knew who would show up for them. He had so many friends come by that it was always a great surprise.

One of the things that always stuck with me is that he treated everyone the same, no matter who it was. Everyone was the same. All he really cared about was that everyone was having a great time and enjoying themselves, and he made certain of that. It didn't matter if it was at Sunday Funday, out at one of the live music venues, at the casino, the local slot bar, a show, my show, or anywhere for that matter.

Couple other quick stories: Vinnie and the Boys went to a home show one day and bought a portable sauna. They all came to the show that night and he asked me if I had one. Of course I didn't—we live in the desert and it's a sauna. Well, a couple days later, I get a note that I have a delivery. What shows up? A sauna. It's still at my house! The other fun story, my assistant Jeff and I were talking about the show when the song, "Send In The Clowns" came on. Not sure why we were listening to that station, but it sparked an idea to have a killer metal version of it. I asked Vinnie if he wanted to be part of it, and he said, "Hellyeah!" We get the time and location set and there's no sign of him. After a few minutes, here comes Vinnie and the boys all dressed in clown costumes, ready to record. He comes in, listens to the rough track and knocked it out of the park on 1 take. The producer asked if he wanted to do a second one to which he replied, "I think we got it, you?" The producer said that it worked by him. He did a song he didn't know in 1 take. That was Vinnie. He didn't have to be the life of the party, he made everyone feel like THEY were!

So, here's to you, Vinnie Paul!

HELLYEAH!!!

-Carrot Top

CHAPTER 1

MAIN

COURSES

BACON-WRAPPED HOT DOGS

"Always a hit at any bash and so simple... BACON MAKES THE WORLD GO AROUND!!!"

INGREDIENTS

1 pack of hot dogs

Cajun seasoning

Bacon

Mustard

Relish

Onions

Shredded cheese

Hot dog buns

1. Let's get to it!!!

2. Take your hot dogs and neatly wrap with bacon.

3. Generously sprinkle Cajun seasoning on hot dogs and toss those bad boys on the grill and grill away.

4. I like to toast my bun on the grill as well, so take toasted bun and squirt mustard on it with some relish and lotsa chopped onions.

5. Add a bacon-wrapped hot dog and cover with shredded cheese and WAHLAH, you just turned a plain ol' hot dog into a redneck gourmet dish!!!

BBQ SAUCED CHEESE BURGERS

"This is a nice spin on a burger – SO GIVE IT A SHOT!!!"

INGREDIENTS

Your favorite BBQ sauce

2 tablespoons of grated apple

2 pounds of ground beef

4 hamburger buns
(split and toasted)

Hamburger pickles

1 sliced red onion

Grated cheddar cheese

Cracked fresh black pepper

1. In a mixing bowl, combine BBQ sauce, apple and fresh cracked pepper.

2. Add ground beef and mix up well.

3. Form into four ½ pound patties.

4. Cook the burgers on uncovered grill for 12-15 minutes, frequently basting with sauce.

5. At the end, add cheddar cheese so it melts!!! Um um good!!!

6. Place burgers on bun and add pickle and onions. Put the top bun on and chow down!!!

LONDON BROIL

"A great steak is hard to beat, so let's take a shot at a BADASS LONDON BROIL!!!"

INGREDIENTS

4 nice cuts of meat

½ cup of olive oil

2 tablespoons of Worcestershire sauce

4 tablespoons of soy sauce

½ cup of lemon juice

1 tablespoon Dijon mustard

4 cloves of garlic

Salt and pepper

Fresh cilantro

1. Ok, let's get this marinade together!!!

2. In a large zip-lock bag, add all ingredients and shake around.

3. Add steak and let marinade for at least 24 hours!!!

4. Heat your grill to high heat. 500° or so. Sear meat on one side for about 2 minutes, then turn meat and cook for another 2-4 minutes depending on how done you want it.

5. Pull the meat, cover with foil and let it sit for about 5 minutes. The meat will continue to cook and the juices will remain in the meat!!!

6. Then fillet and serve!!!

7. Cheers!!!

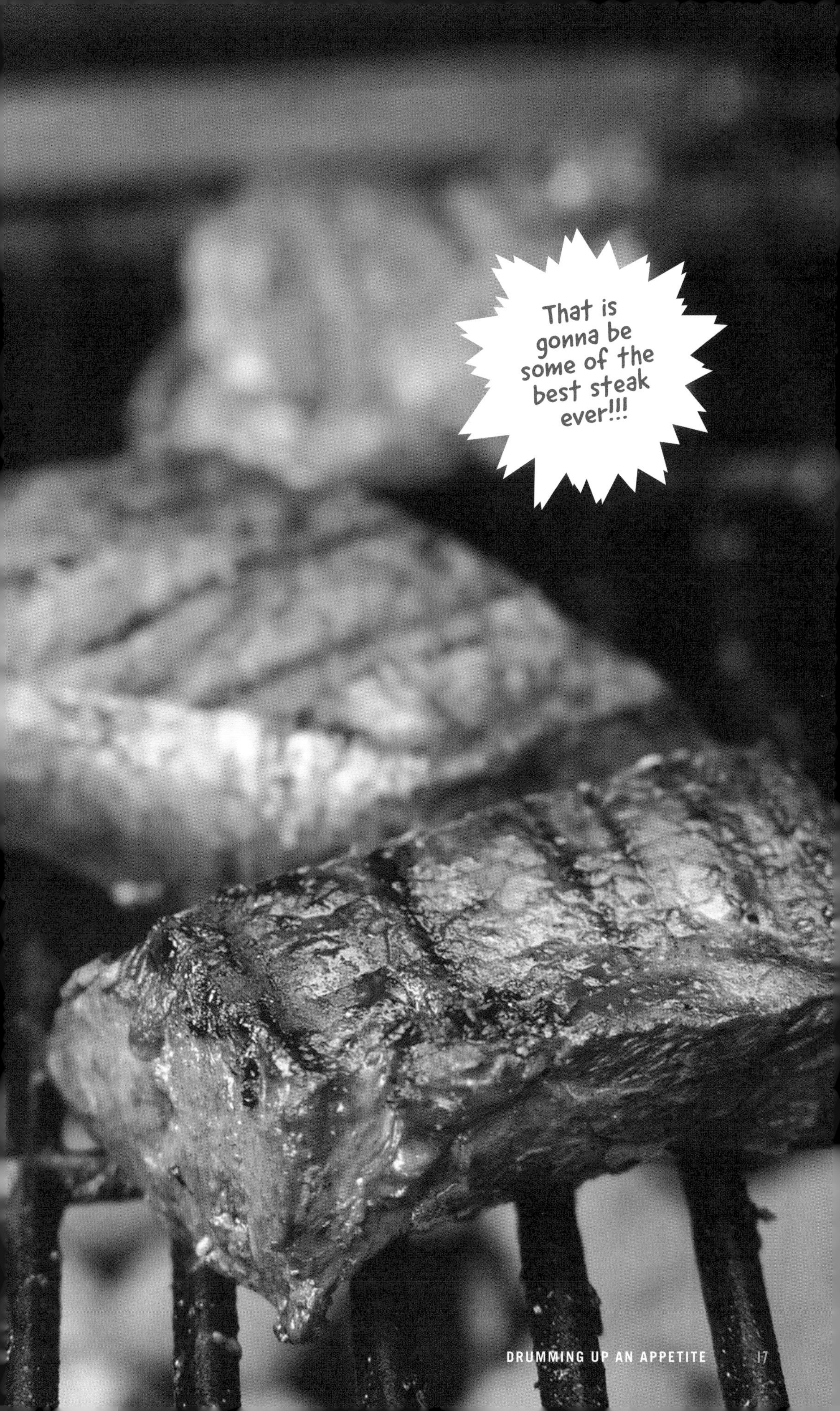
That is gonna be some of the best steak ever!!!

Truly underrated!!!

PORKIN' PORK CHOPS

"THESE BABIES ARE SO UNDERRATED, yet so damn good and easy to make and always a hit at any BBQ!!!"

INGREDIENTS

Thin-sliced pork chops

Worcestershire sauce

Montréal steak seasoning

Your favorite BBQ sauce

1. So easy!!! Fire up the grill and let's get these finger-lickin'-good bad boys on the grill!!!

2. Take your pork chops and cover with Worcestershire sauce and then cover with Montréal seasoning and let 'em set for 30 minutes. Toss on the hot grill and cook for 2-4 minutes on each side… THAT'S IT!!!

3. You might wanna hit 'em with your favorite BBQ sauce for added enjoyment!!!

4. HELLYEAH!!!

RANCH STEAK

**"This is a kickass Southern style steak!!!
TRUST ME ON THIS, IT ROCKS!!!"**

INGREDIENTS

Badass lean sirloin

Chipotle Cholula

Ranch dressing

Fajita seasoning

Fritos chips

Heinz 57 sauce

1. Finely crush Fritos and I mean CRUSH THEM.

2. Add a ton of Cholula, then add enough ranch dressing to make you happy. Mix it all up and massage liberally into your steak.

3. Hit 'em with some fajita seasoning, then toss on a hot grill for about 3 or 4 minutes per side.

4. When these bad boys come off the grill, you will be amazed!!!

5. If you want some extra flair, hit 'em with some HEINZ 57 SAUCE!!!

6. WOOO HOOOOO!!!

TEXAS STYLE PHILLY CHEESE STEAK SAMMICH

"THIS IS MY TWIST ON A PHILLY CHEESE STEAK. After havin' many famous cheese steaks in the city of brotherly love, I was always disappointed that they never lived up to the cheese steaks my mom used to make, so I had to include this with all the fixin's!!!"

INGREDIENTS

1 Box Steak-umm sliced steaks (these are the best for cheese steaks around, but others can be substituted)

1 diced white onion

1 diced red onion

1 diced green bell pepper

1 diced red bell pepper

1 diced yellow bell pepper

1 can diced green olives

1 can diced black olives

1 can diced mushrooms

1 jar banana peppers

1 jar chopped garlic

Olive oil

Sliced provolone cheese

Your favorite hoagie buns

Salt & pepper

1. Football's on the big screen and the beer is cold!!! It's a party and everyone is hungry!!!

2. HELLYEAH!!! Let's get busy!!!

3. Fire up a flat grill. Now, each Philly is made to order, so I set all the ingredients beside the grill so each person can see what's available. You will also need a good long and wide spatula to turn the Philly's.

4. Start by puttin' some olive oil on the grill and add some chopped garlic. Then start with all the veggies first. I like it all, so put some peppers, mushrooms, olives, onions and lotsa banana peppers on.

5. Salt and pepper and move around until all the veggies are grilled up.

6. Then put 2 Steak-umm's on. After meat is browned, mix it with veggies and make a thick straight line... lay 2 pieces of provolone cheese on top and cover with your hoagie bun. Let cook for about 2 minutes until cheese is melted.

7. Now, this is the trick... quickly slide your spatula under the cheese steak and flip it over and plate it!!! There you have it!!!

8. Guaranteed to put a smile on everyone's faces, but watch out... you might miss the game being in the kitchen all day!!! Especially if they keep comin' back for more like MONGO!!! He ate 10 at one Super Bowl!!!

9. GO COWBOYS!!!

WORLD FAMOUS GRILLED PEANUT BUTTER JALAPEÑOS!!!

"These are a big hit at my HELLYEAH BBQs and so easy to make, so FIRE UP YOUR GRILL!!!"

INGREDIENTS

24 fresh jalapeños

1 large jar of your favorite peanut butter

1 bag of Fritos chips

1 bag of real bacon bits

1 bag of shredded Mexican cheese

1 bottle of your favorite grape jelly

1. Take the jalapeños and cut in half long-wise. Then, take a spoon and scoop out the veins and seeds. Spoon in the peanut butter. Now, sprinkle your bacon bits on these bad boys!!!

2. Here comes the kicker: take the Fritos and crush them in the bag and then sprinkle it on the jalapeños. Finally, you cover them with the shredded cheese!!! Put them on a medium hot grill and close the lid to melt the cheese. Keep an eye on them and when the jalapeños get a nice char on them and the cheese is melted, they are done!!!

3. Pull 'em off the grill and hit 'em with your grape jelly and you are in for a treat that is really different and excites all your taste buds!!!

Rock it!!!

BADASS BLT

"This is really simple and there is some kind of chemical in bacon that cures hangovers... SO AFTER A NIGHT OF HARD DRINKIN', FIRE ONE OF THESE BADASS BLTS UP AND START ALL OVER AGAIN!!! Remember a hangover is inspiration!!! HELLYEAH!!!"

HERE'S WHATCHA NEED PER SANDWICH:

4 slices of bacon

Mayonnaise

Sliced beefsteak tomato

Romaine lettuce

Your favorite bread
(I like wheat!!!)

Butter

Fresh cracked pepper

...and a sliced white onion
(optional)

1. Cook your bacon in a fryin' pan at a medium high heat.

2. I like my bacon crispy, so cook it till you like it.

3. Toast your bread and spread butter on it.

4. Spread mayonnaise on it after butter melts.

5. Stack bacon, lettuce, tomato.
   (and I like sliced onion as well...)

6. then crack some black pepper on that BADASS BLT and chow down!!!

7. These babies ROCK and are good anytime (and cheap too!!!)

LOBSTER TEXAS STYLE

"This might throw you Northerners for a loop, but lobster just gets ruined when you boil it. THAT'S RIGHT, I SAID IT GETS RUINED!!! Let me show ya how to get the best flavor and texture outta your lobster!!!"

INGREDIENTS

4 nice lobster tails

Olive oil

Montréal steak seasoning

1 large lemon

1 stick of butter

Minced garlic

1. Take your lobster tails outta the shell, or if you like the shell for show, cut it open down the middle of the back and expose the meat leavin' it connected to the end of the shell. Put 'em in a plastic bag with olive oil and Montréal steak seasoning and let marinade for about a hour.

2. Fire up your grill on high and make sure to add some of your favorite wet wood to give it a smoky flavor (I like mesquite or hickory). Toss the lobster on the grill and cook for about 2-3 minutes each side. Then pull 'em off the grill. Melt your butter with lemon squeezed in it and minced garlic… dip your lobster as usual.

3. That grilled lobster owns boiled lobster, you will see!!!

4. That's amazing lobster, Texas style!!! HELLYEAH!!!

You're gonna need a Crockpot to make these and you will be able to use it all the time, so it's a great investment!!!

ROCKIN' PORK TACOS

"These rule and are easy to make."

INGREDIENTS

1 pound pork roast

1 medium onion, sliced

1 red bell pepper, sliced

1 habanero pepper, finely chopped

1 bottle of Hawaiian marinade

Chipotle Cholula

1 tablespoon minced garlic

1 tablespoon cumin

1 tablespoon chili powder

1 chopped white onion

1 lime

1. Place your ingredients in a Crockpot and cook for at least 4 hours!!!

2. Shred the pork with a fork and serve on your favorite hard or soft tortillas.

3. Top 'em with your favorite taco toppings, or them spirits with a lime wedge and add a generous amount of Chipotle Cholula!!!

CHAPTER 2
SIDES

AND APPS

AVOCADO & CORN SALSA

"THIS IS A GREAT TWIST ON REGULAR GUACAMOLE AND IS SURE TO BE A HIT!!!"

INGREDIENTS

1 cup of corn

Minced garlic

1 cup quartered grape tomatoes

2 medium avocados diced

Chopped fresh cilantro

2 teaspoons lime juice

Kosher salt

1. Toss avocados, corn, tomatoes, cilantro, lime juice, garlic and salt in a medium bowl.

2. That's it... that was easy!!!!

3. Eat with your favorite tortilla chips or I like it with Fritos!!!

4. Great for parties and tailgating!!

5. Enjoy!!!

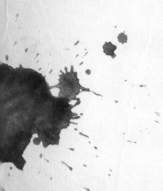

BBQ BAKED BEANS

"EASY TO MAKE, AND GOES GREAT WITH EVERYTHING!!!"

INGREDIENTS

1 big can baked beans

1 jar minced garlic

1 chopped white onion

1 sliced jalapeño

1 sliced green bell pepper

Ketchup

Your favorite BBQ sauce

Sliced bacon

Montréal steak seasoning

1. In a baking dish, add beans.

2. Then mix in some minced garlic, chopped onions and line the top with sliced jalapeños and green bell peppers.

3. Then cover with sliced bacon and pour ketchup on top.

4. Swirl BBQ sauce on top.

5. Finally, sprinkle Montréal steak seasoning on top, then put in a 400° oven and bake for about 25 minutes and look out!!!

One of the best side dishes ever!!! Em em good!!!

BERRY SUMMER SALAD

"This salad is incredible and super healthy and great on a hot summer day. So head to your fresh open-air market, **PICK UP SOME PRODUCE AND ENJOY."**

INGREDIENTS

Raspberries

Blueberries

Cranberries

Strawberries

Blue cheese

Pecans

Iceberg lettuce

Chopped cucumber

Chopped tomatoes

Ranch dressing

1. Toss the lettuce, tomatoes, cucumber and berries up in a bowl.

2. Then sprinkle the blue cheese and pecans on top.

3. Then hit it with your ranch dressing!!! Yummy and super refreshing!!!

4. You can also add a grilled chicken breast or grilled shrimp to make a fuller meal. Cheers!!!

Let's explode!!!

CHERRY BOMBS

**"This is a mighty fine appetizer that's so easy to make.
You will be blown away!!!
LITERALLY, BLOWN AWAY WITH CHERRY BOMBS!!!"**

INGREDIENTS

Cherry tomatoes

Cream cheese

Avocado

Habanero peppers

Paprika

1. Let's get these explosive bad boys ready to blow your taste buds away!!!

2. Take your cherry tomatoes and cut in half. With a baby spoon, scoop the insides out into a bowl. Mix the tomato pulp with the cream cheese. Stuff each cherry tomato half with the cream cheese mixture.

3. Then, take an avocado and dice it up. Place on top of each cherry tomato. Now here comes the fun part. Take a habanero and julienne it, then place one in each cherry tomato sticking out like a fuse.

4. These are the BOMB and will be a hit anytime anywhere!!! Here comes the BOOM!!! CHERRY BOMBS!!!

CRAZY CORN

**"I LEARNED THIS RECIPE FROM A MIDGET THAT WAS IN A CIRCUS!!!
This will make you wanna work for the circus –
CAUSE IT'S CRAZY!!!"**

INGREDIENTS

**Corn on the cob, shucked
(however many you need!!!)**

Mayonnaise

Cajun seasoning

Limes

1. Take your corn on the cob and spread mayonnaise on it. Then, sprinkle Cajun seasoning on it liberally.

2. Wrap those ears in foil, then put on a hot grill and rotate every 5-10 minutes for about a hour.

3. Take out of the foil and squeeze lime juice on 'em and chow down. You will be goin' crazy!!! It's soooooooooo bangin'!!! That's why it's crazy corn!!!

BLACK SABBATH SHRIMP!!!

*"WELL!!! THE GREATEST HEAVY METAL BAND EVER,
I made this shrimp in honor of them!!!
(OZZY, YOU GOTTA TRY THIS!!!)
I jammed with them but never got to cook for them!!!"*

INGREDIENTS

**Shrimp!!! BIG 'UNS!!! (10-20)
no shell, deveined**

Black pepper

Habanero peppers

Olive oil

Parmesan cheese

1. Marinate your huge shrimp in olive oil, chopped habanero peppers and tons of fresh cracked black pepper!!! (3 hours at least!!!)

2. Then, put in a 400° oven for 15 minutes!!!

3. Sprinkle generously with parmesan cheese and if you're serious about heat, add Tabasco or your favorite hot sauce!!!

4. The heat is sure to make you PARANOID!!!

This soup is a winner!!!

CREAM OF ROASTED RED PEPPER AND TOMATO SOUP

"OK!!! A sure favorite hit with all soup lovers...
It's simple to make and goes great with a
BLT sammich or grilled cheese sammich!!!
So, here we go... Let's fire one up and get on it.
YOU'LL HAVE THE MUNCHIES IN NO TIME!!! HELLYEAH!!!"

INGREDIENTS

2 large cans (20 ounces) puréed or stewed tomatoes

2 large red bell peppers

Chopped fresh basil

½ stick of butter

Fresh cracked black pepper

1 lemon

2 cups of fresh cream

Parmesan

Chopped green scallions

1. Fire up your grill!!! Take your red peppers and cut those bad boys open. Scoop all the seeds out, then rub them in some olive oil and hit with some salt and pepper!!!

2. Toss 'em on the grill and char them. Lots of chefs clean the charred skin off, but that's where that roasted flavor is, so leave all that good stuff on there!!! Get your Crockpot and put on high heat. Add peppers and your tomatoes. Add chopped basil along with the half or whole stick of butter depending on how rich you like it!!! Sprinkle fresh cracked pepper and cook for about 2 hours. Stir in cream and squeeze in lemon juice, then purée to the thickness you desire.

3. When serving, add parmesan cheese and chopped green scallions... Watch out!!! This is a winner!!! You can set it up before you go out partying and when you get back and you are all buzzed up, you got something that blows Denny's or Jack-in-the-Box away!!!

VINNIE PAUL'S WORLD FAMOUS STUFFED JALAPEÑOS

**"ALL RIGHT BROTHERS AND SISTERS...
HERE IT IS!!! MY SIGNATURE DISH!!!**
I have served these to just about every rockstar and celebrity on the face of the earth, and I always get a unanimous thumbs up!!! It's easy, and everyone craves more...
**(NOT TO MENTION THEY WILL BE REMINDED
THE NEXT DAY HOW GOOD THEY WERE!!!)**
Let's get goin', shall we?"

INGREDIENTS

A dozen fresh jalapeños

Philadelphia cream cheese

Shredded Mexican cheese

Fajita or taco seasoning

Your favorite BBQ sauce
(*I like Jack Daniels' Old No. 7 BBQ sauce!!!*)

1. Take your fresh green jalapeños and cut in half long ways. Get a spoon and scrape the seeds out, that's where the excessive heat is and you need the room in there anyways!!!

2. Get your cream cheese and stuff the jalapeños with a spoon. Then sprinkle with some fajita or taco seasoning... or hell, *both* if you like!!! Then cover with some shredded Mexican cheese.

3. Now, throw those bad boys on your grill. Cook those bad boys till they are charred and the cheese is melted, then take off.

4. Now, here is the kicker!!! Top with your favorite BBQ sauce and serve. There's nothin' like the heat from the pepper along with the cream cheese and the sweetness of the BBQ sauce!!!

Hellyeah!!!!
This is great
at parties, BBQs
and all drinkin'
occasions!!

LEMON PEPPER CHICKEN WINGS

**"Most people think if you say wings,
YOU'RE TALKIN' HOT AND SPICY!!!
Well, here's a new twist they will love!!!"**

INGREDIENTS

2 dozen chicken wings/drums

1 stick of butter

1 lemon

Lemon pepper

Salt and pepper

Ranch or blue cheese
(optional)

Celery and carrot strips
(optional)

1. Take your chicken wings and sprinkle salt and pepper on them. Then, toss on a hot grill and turn them every 2 minutes or so, until they are nice and crispy.

2. Take a mixing bowl and microwave your butter to liquid. Squeeze lemon juice on your butter, then take the cooked wings and mix them all around in the butter and lemon juice!!! Sprinkle lemon pepper all over them…

3. Serve with ranch or blue cheese and with lotsa celery and carrot strips!!!

4. HELLYEAH!!!

MAGIC ORIENTAL MUSHROOMS

"THESE ARE AMAZING WHEN YOU GOT A BUZZ!!!"

INGREDIENTS

Fresh mushrooms, stems removed

Owen's Sausage

Fresh sliced jalapeños

1 jar minced garlic

Fresh ginger

Teriyaki sauce

1. Take the mushrooms and place on a cookie sheet. Put 1 slice of jalapeño and 1/4 teaspoon of minced garlic in each. THEN TAKE YOUR FRESH GINGER AND PUT A SMALL SLICE IN EACH!!!

2. Then stuff with sausage and bake at 400° for about 15 minutes!!!

3. Pull 'em out and cover with your Teriyaki sauce, then put back in oven to caramelize them for another 5-10 minutes... That's it!!!

4. Appetizers are a huge hit and these are one of my favorites!!!

FRIED ZUCCHINI

"PARTY TIME HERE!!! I grow my own zucchini, so this is double-special to me!!!"

INGREDIENTS

Fresh zucchini, sliced

2 eggs

flour

Cajun seasoning

Ranch dressing
(or your favorite dipping sauce)

1. Take your eggs and put 'em in a mixing bowl. Whisk around nicely. In another bowl, add flour and lotsa Cajun seasoning.

2. Fire your deep fryer up on hot or use a fryin' pan with olive oil. Take the sliced zucchini and dip it in egg wash then toss 'em around in flour. Drop 'em in the deep fryer or the pan and cook!!! It takes 2-5 minutes. Pull 'em out and place on paper towels to absorb excessive grease.

3. Dip in ranch dressing or your favorite dipping sauce and you're in heaven!!!

4. HELLYEAH!!!

Keep it simple!!!

JALAPEÑO CORN BREAD

"This goes great with anything... ESPECIALLY BAKED BEANS AND HAM!!!"

INGREDIENTS

Jiffy Corn Bread Mix
(and the called-for ingredients on the box)

8 small jalapeños

1 can Green Giant golden corn

3 cups of grated cheese

1 chopped white onion

1. Mix all ingredients in a bowl.

2. Pour the mixture into muffin pans and bake about 15 minutes at 410°.

3. Always keep an eye on any kind of bread, last thing you wanna do is burn it!!!

KALE & CHERRY SALAD

"THIS IS THE BEST AND HEALTHIEST SALAD I'VE EVER MADE!!! Absolutely killer and it will make you feel all good about yourself cause it's so tasty (but healthy!!!) Let's get our greens on!!!"

INGREDIENTS

Fresh kale (and **LOTS** of it)

Fresh cherries, pitted and sliced

Fresh baby grape tomatoes

1 sliced jalapeño

Sliced red onion

Sliced cucumber

Bacon bits

Grated cheddar cheese

Fresh pecans

Montréal steak seasoning

Your favorite vinaigrette
(I like Panera bread company balsamic vinaigrette)

1. Like any salad, toss all your goodies!!!

2. Serve and you & your guest can add your favorite vinaigrette!!!

3. This is so easy, healthy and real winner!!!

4. Cheers!!!

SLAMMIN' DEVILED EGGS

"You can make these babies ahead of time and they are a great party appetizer or great for football parties... And of course late-night munchies!!! LET'S START THE SHOW!!!"

INGREDIENTS

1 dozen eggs

Mayonnaise

Mustard

Hot dog relish

1 small jar of pimento peppers

Montréal steak seasoning

Paprika

Tabasco or Cholula (optional)

1. Let's start by boiling your eggs... be sure and add salt to your water!!! Boil for about 15-20 minutes, then rinse with cold water.

2. Let cool for about 20 minutes, then crack and peel shells. Slice each egg once long-wise.

3. Take the cooked yolk and put in a mixing bowl... Do this to all eggs... place those eggs on a serving tray. Now, take your mixing bowl with the yolks and add even parts mayonnaise and mustard, then add relish, Montréal steak seasoning and pimento peppers. Mix it up to whatever consistency you like. I like mine about mashed potatoes consistency.

4. OK, here is the cool part but it's tricky... Get a plastic sandwich bag and cut ½ inch off one of the corners and then fill it with the egg filling. Squeeze the plastic bag from the top down like a pastry bag and you fill each egg!!!

5. Sprinkle paprika for color and heat on each egg and chill!!! These babies are ready to rock!!!

6. HELLYEAH!!! You might even hit 'em with some Tabasco or Cholula when you serve 'em if you like 'em kicked up!!!

PAN-FRIED PEPPERS

"These are for people who like it hawt!!! I MEAN HOT!!!"

INGREDIENTS

Whole jalapeño peppers

Olive oil

Fajita seasoning

1. Watch out!!! Pan-frying jalapeños increases the heat about 1000%!!!

2. So, take a fryin' pan and on high heat, add some olive oil. Toss your peppers in and hit with a bunch of fajita seasoning. With tongs, keep turning the peppers. Cook 'em till nice and charred all over. Caliente!!! Great with steaks, fish, chops and for any one who loves the rush of eating hot peppers!!!

3. HELLYEAH!!!

4. OH, make sure you got a cold glass of spirits around to put your mouth out!!!

I'd like to thank Carolyn Abbott for this recipe!!!

MY MOM'S FAMOUS PEA SALAD

"THIS WAS ALWAYS A HIT AT THANKSGIVING AND CHRISTMAS. My mom loved to cook and this was one of her best dishes. Everyone is always askin' for it and I did my best to do my Mama proud and carry on the tradition, so here we go!!!"

INGREDIENTS

2 bags of frozen English green peas

1 jar of Miracle Whip (my mom always insisted on it instead of plain ol' mayonnaise)

1 chopped white onion

2 hard boiled eggs

1 box of Velveeta cheese

1 small bottle of pimento peppers

1 lemon

Fresh cracked black pepper

1. Ok let's rock this badass salad!!!

2. Get a large salad bowl. Thaw the green peas and put 'em in the bowl. Add mayonnaise. Chop up your white onion and add that. Slice your Velveeta cheese into bit-size blocks and add those.

3. Then take your hard-boiled eggs and dice them up and add 'em.

4. Toss your pimento peppers in and squeeze your lemon into the bowl and mix that baby up!!!

5. Let set in refrigerator, then serve.

6. Add black pepper to taste.

7. This is a great holiday dish, or any other time of the year!!!

8. HELLYEAH!!!

SPICY HELLYEAH PICKLES

"Now... I love pickles and these are kicked up a notch and will light you up!!!
REALLY SIMPLE, SO LET'S GET 'EM GOIN'!!!"

INGREDIENTS

1 cup vinegar

1/2 cup Kosher salt

3 garlic cloves

2 cucumbers

1 chopped habanero pepper

Hot sauce (I prefer Cholula!!!)

1. Mix your vinegar and salt until that salt is dissolved!!! Crush the garlic and add to vinegar brine.

2. Add hot sauce 'till you obtain desired heat.

3. Slice cucumbers and SOAK in brine. Let 'em soak for at least one hour.

4. Refrigerate for up to three weeks. The longer the better they get!!!

5. HELLYEAH!!!

TOMATILLO & HABANERO SAUCE

"THIS IS NOT FOR THE FAINT AT HEART OR HEAT PUSSIES!!!
For real!!! Let's get the heat blazin'!!!
HELLYEAH!!!"

INGREDIENTS

10 tomatillos

10 habanero peppers

5 garlic cloves

Cilantro

1 lime

White vinegar

Montréal steak seasoning

Olive oil

1. Take your tomatillos and habaneros and quarter them and put 'em in a baking dish along with garlic cloves and hit with some olive oil and Montréal steak seasoning!!!

2. Roast 'em in the oven at 400° 'till it's nice and charred. Lotsa people peel the charred skin, but I like it because it adds a nice smoky charred flavor to the sauce, so leave it on!!!

3. Once it's out of the oven, put it in a blender and add cilantro, a bit of vinegar and squeeze the lime in and hit purée!!!

4. This sauce is a hit on those cold days watchin' football and it will light your friends on fire!!! You can also make this sauce with regular red tomatoes to make more of a habenero hot sauce!!! I like to make 'em both!!!

5. Cheers!!!

WAILIN' WATERMELON SALSA

"This is a wild one, but a killer summertime change of pace. TRY THIS WITH ALL MEXICAN FOOD... IT'S DIFFERENT!!!"

INGREDIENTS

2 cups diced watermelon

1 cup diced white onion

2 chopped fresh jalapeño peppers

2 tablespoons olive oil

2 teaspoons apple cider vinegar

1 fresh lime

Salt and pepper

½ cup finely chopped cilantro

1. In a large mixing bowl, combine all ingredients!!!

2. Mix 'em well and chill overnight!!!

3. Squeeze the lime juice and serve with chips, in tacos or whatever...

4. Your friends will love this!!!

FIRED-UP ROASTED CORN CHOWDER

"I love this soup and it's great in the winter, but just as good in the summer!!! The sweetness of the corn and the heat from the sriracha rocks your world like no other!!! SO, LET'S GET IT ON!!!"

INGREDIENTS

4 ears of sweet corn

1 diced red bell pepper

1 diced red onion

Minced garlic

4 cans of chicken stock

½ cup sriracha sauce

1 cup warm heavy cream

Fresh cilantro

Olive oil

1. Fire up your grill and baste your corn ears with butter or olive oil and hit 'em with some salt and pepper!!! Throw those bad boys on the grill and roast 'em up good until you get a nice black char goin'. Remove from grill and cut the kernels off the cob and set 'em aside.

2. Heat up a soup pan on medium heat and add olive oil, bell pepper, onion, garlic and sweat for 10 minutes.

3. Then add roasted corn, sriracha, and chicken stock and bring to a boil. Then, stir in the warm heavy cream and as much cilantro as you like.

4. Cook for another 10 minutes and you're ready to rock!!! You can add more sriracha if you feel the need for heat in your seat!!!

5. Haha, it's delicious!!! Now you're all fired up!!!

STUFFED MUSHROOMS

INGREDIENTS

**Fresh mushrooms,
stems removed**

Owen's Sausage

Fresh sliced jalepeños

1 jar minced garlic

Parmesan cheese

1. Take mushrooms and place on a cookie sheet.

2. Put 1 slice of jalapeño in each and a 1/4 teaspoon of minced garlic in each, then stuff with sausage!!!

3. Bake at 400° for about 20 minutes, then sprinkle with parmesan cheese!!!

These are amazing appetizers, a huge hit!!!

CHAPTER 3
DESSERTS

EVIL BBQ BAKED APPLES

"OH BOY, WATCH OUT!!!
These are a one-of-a-kind and I highly
recommend you try this at home...
Nothing else like it!!!"

INGREDIENTS

6 apples,
cored 2/3rds through

Hot Tamales candy

Cinnamon

Sugar

1. Fill each apple with Hot Tamales.

2. Wrap in aluminum foil, poke with a fork a few times.

3. Bake at 400° for about 1 hour.

4. Peel foil and sprinkle with cinnamon and sugar and enjoy your evil desert!!!

5. I love these!!!

ORANGE CRAZE

"THIS IS AN EASY AND VERY DIFFERENT ONE I CAME UP WITH LATE AT NIGHT WITH A KILLER BUZZ GOIN'!!!
It's really simple and takes 2 minutes to make and you won't believe how tasty it is, so let's get Orange Crazy!!"

INGREDIENTS

Oranges

Tabasco sauce

Montréal steak seasoning

1. Peel the oranges and break 'em into slices. Then DOUSE them in Tabasco sauce!!!

2. Sprinkle Montréal steak seasoning on them and guess what? You got Orange Craze!!!

3. I know it sounds bizarre, but it's amazing!!!

BIG EASY BANANA PUDDING

"This is so easy, a 5-year-old could make it and so delicious, EVERYONE is going to want your recipe!!! JUST TELL 'EM VINNIE TOLD YA... HAHA."

INGREDIENTS

2 boxes instant vanilla pudding mix

Milk

6 bananas, chopped

1 box Nilla Wafers

1. Take your vanilla pudding and mix with hot milk according to the directions on the box.

2. Get a mixing bowl... Preferably a glass see-thru one so people can see what you have created!!! Line the mixing bowl with Nilla Wafers, then chopped bananas and then pour some pudding in!!! Repeat 2 or 3 times till full.

3. Then crush up about 10 Nilla Wafers and sprinkle 'em on top nice and purdy!!! Put in refrigerator for a few hours and serve!!!

LOW-CARB CHEESECAKE

*"This low-carb, no-bake cheesecake is easy to make,
and you can top it in many different ways.
(The crust does require a few minutes in the oven,
but you can also serve it crustless; see note below)
The easiest is to spread a jar of sugar-free jam over it.
This would add about 2 grams of carbs per serving to
the basic cheesecake. Other options are to cover with
fresh fruit in season, or simply cook frozen berries
with sweetener to taste until thickened.
The cheesecake pictured here was made in
this way with frozen strawberries."*

INGREDIENTS

1 low-carb pie crust

**10oz. cream cheese,
room temperature**

2 teaspoons vanilla extract

1 teaspoon lemon juice

Zero-carb sugar substitute
(equal to about ½ cup sugar,
or to taste)

1 cup heavy cream

1. Bake the low-carb pie crust in a deep-dish pie pan.

2. Mix cream cheese, vanilla, lemon juice, and sugar substitute very well. If you are using an electric mixer, fluff it up for a minute or two.

3. In a second bowl, whip the cream to soft peaks - you actually want it slightly less beaten than you would for a dessert topping.

4. Mix about a third of the whipped cream into the cream cheese mixture. Then gently mix another third in, and then the rest. Spread cream cheese mixture into crust. Smooth it off and chill for at least 2-3 hours. Cover with topping and serve.

5. With crust, each serving has 3.5 grams of carbs. Without, it's 2 grams of carbs. Amazing!!! Eat good and lose weight!!! A seriously cool concept!!!

6. (Crustless option: Chill cream cheese mixture in bowl, and then serve in individual dishes with topping.)

The crust is my easy low-carb pie crust on the next page, so do that first!!!

LOW-CARB PIECRUST

"THIS IS A VERY EASY PIECRUST TO MAKE!!!
This works best for a 9" pie pan.
If you have an 8" one, the crust will be a little thicker,
or you can cut back on the ingredients a bit."

INGREDIENTS

1½ cups almond meal or almond flour

3 tablespoons melted butter

**Artificial sweetener
(equal to 3 tablespoons of sugar)**

1. Heat oven to 350°. Melt the butter (if your pie pan is microwave safe, melt the butter in it!!!) and mix the ingredients up in the pan and pat into place with your fingertips.

2. Bake for about 10 minutes until the crust is beginning to brown. After 8 minutes, check every minute or so, because once it starts to brown it goes quickly!!! The whole pie shell has 11 grams of carbs, and tastes as good as a pie crust with 70 or 80 grams.

3. That's the bomb!!!

BEST HAWAIIAN DESSERT I EVER MADE

"This is a kick in the ass, with a nice sweet side... LIKE HAVING GOOD SEX!!! It doesn't get any better, so let's do this!!!"

INGREDIENTS

1 or 2 cans of sliced pineapples
(depending on how many guests - I'm thinkin' 2 cause it's a party!!!)

Coconut milk

Brown sugar

Cinnamon

Fresh green jalapeño

Toothpicks

1. Like I said, I love this and everyone who's ever had it freaks the fuck out!!!

2. Take sliced pineapples and marinate in coconut milk. Generously sprinkle cinnamon and brown sugar all over them. Slice fresh jalapeños and place on top of pineapples with toothpicks.

3. Grill covered 'till charred... OMG!!!!!

4. I'm not really a dessert dude, but this is the bomb!!!

5. If you really wanna kill it, add a scoop of vanilla ice cream!!!

6. FUCK!!!

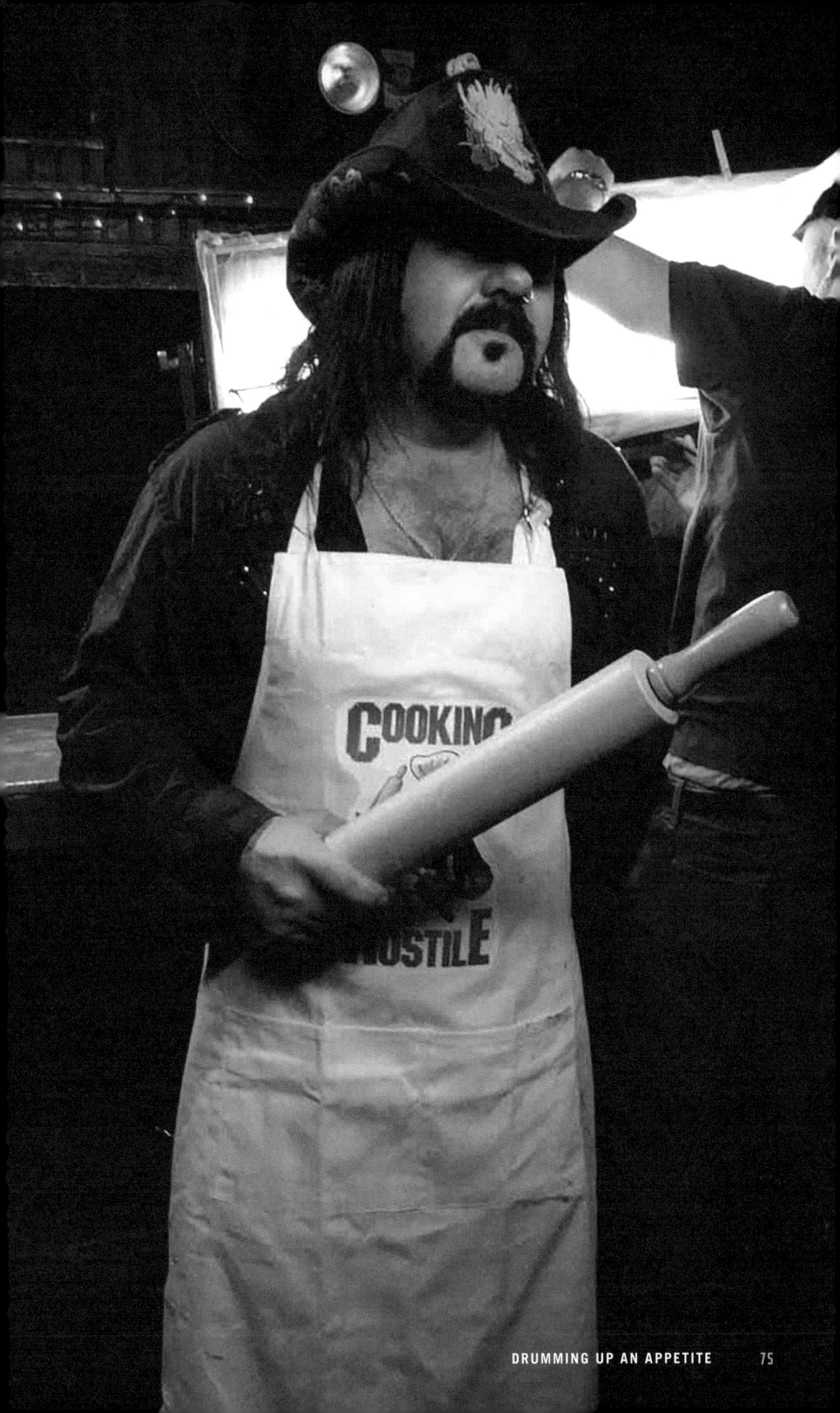
COOKING